LAVA BLAZE 2

USER MANUAL

GUIDE

The Comprehensive Guide to Unlocking Every Feature, Tips & Tricks, Troubleshooting Secrets & Unleashing Its full Potential.

Carl Steven

All Rights Reserved.

No part of this book may be used or reproduced by any means, graphic, electronic, or mechanical, including photocopying, recording, taping, or by any information storage retrieval system without the written permission of the publisher.

Copyright © 2022 by **Carl Steven**

TABLE OF CONTENT

Chapter One

Ignite Your Sparks

Welcome to the Inferno

Brace yourself, tech adventurer, for the Lava Blaze 2 is not only a phone; rather, it is a raging fire of possibilities that are just waiting to be released. This is not only an update; rather, it is a raging volcano of cutting-edge technology that is prepared to transform the digital environment you are now experiencing.

Imagine a gadget that marries a beautiful design with powerful power. A phone that smoothly interacts with your life, anticipating your needs before you ever articulate them. That's the Lava Blaze 2. Its blazing-fast CPU explodes with speed, tackling difficult tasks like a dragon devours its prey. The display, a brilliant canvas of color and clarity, delivers every picture with astonishing detail. What about the battery? What a battery that is! Because it is a legendary beast that lives for a longer period than a phoenix, you will be able to maintain your connections and productivity without the continual worry of an energy breakdown.

On the other hand, the Lava Blaze 2 is not just about figures and specifications. Defying expectations and pushing the limits of what is possible are both important. It's the phone that allows you to capture the world in breathtaking clarity with its multi-lens camera system, and then share your flaming creations with lightning-fast connection. It's the phone that enhances your productivity with its easy UI and powerful applications, letting you tackle your to-do list like a dragon tamer. It's the phone that keeps you amused with intense gaming, crystal-clear streaming, and a library of unlimited possibilities.

This isn't just a phone; it's an extension of yourself, a doorway to a world of unlimited possibilities. It's the Lava Blaze 2, and it's ready to fire your digital life.

Here's a peek at the blazing characteristics that await:

- Blazing-fast Processor: Power through tough activities like a dragon devours a feast.
- Vivid Display: Immerse yourself in a world of brilliant colors and remarkable clarity.

- Epic Battery Life: Stay connected and productive without worry of the dreaded power decline.

- Multi-Lens Camera System: Capture amazing photographs and films that will leave you stunned.

- Lightning-Fast Connectivity: Share your flaming masterpieces with the world in a wink.

- Intuitive Interface: Conquer your to-do list with ease and efficiency.

- Immersive Gaming: Experience gaming like never before, with visuals that will melt your face.

- Endless Entertainment: Stream, listen, play, and explore — the options are infinite.

This is only the beginning, dear explorer. The Lava Blaze 2 is your entryway to a digital inferno, eager to be explored. So, grab your phone, take a deep breath, and be ready to be engulfed by the fires of invention.

The journey begins now.

First Contact: Igniting Your Lava Blaze 2

Congratulations! You've just taken home the Lava Blaze 2, a smartphone ready to ignite with promise. But before you release its blazing force, let's take time to develop a bond. This is your guide to the initial setup, navigating the UI, and making critical adjustments to properly own your Lava Blaze 2 as your own.

Power Up!

Plug your Lava Blaze 2 into its charger and behold the power button turns into a pulsing ember. Press it, and see your screen burst to life with the Lava Blaze 2 logo, a fitting herald of the tech inferno you're about to enter.

Language of Fire:

Choose your chosen language, the one that will whisper instructions and interpret the digital whispers of the internet. English, Hindi, Spanish? The Lava Blaze 2 speaks to them all.

Connecting to the Network:

Now, let's connect to the lifeblood of the digital world: Wi-Fi. Select your network, input the password, and watch as your Lava Blaze 2 joins the digital dance floor. Don't worry, if you're out in the wild, mobile data is only a touch away.

Google's Guiding Hand:

Next, you'll discover the familiar face of Google Play Services. Sign in or create an account, and access a realm of applications, games, and unlimited possibilities. Think of it as your passport to the digital sphere.

Time to Shine:

Personalize your home screen! Choose a wallpaper that sets your spirit flame, whether it's a flaming countryside or a tranquil ocean. Arrange your favorite programs like constellations, ready to be touched with a touch.

Essential Tweaks:

Dive into the Settings section, your laboratory for fine-tuning your Lava Blaze 2. Adjust brightness, set auto-lock timings, and tune noises and alerts to your taste. Make it an extension of your personality, a mirror of your digital self.

Welcome to the Inferno:

Congratulations! You've successfully managed your Lava Blaze 2's initial encounter. Now, explore its characteristics, dig into its secret depths, and let your creativity emerge. Remember, this is only the beginning of your burning adventure.

Demystifying the Dashboard: A Deep Dive into Your Lava Blaze 2's Control Center

Imagine your Lava Blaze 2 as a burning volcano. The home screen is the crater rim, allowing spectacular views and easy access to the most explosive elements. Quick settings are the secret fumaroles, bursting with handy modifications. And the notification center? Well, let's just say it's where the ash lands, keeping you informed of any eruptions — both actual and figurative.

Home Screen: Your Fiery Command Center

Picture your home screen as a unique lava flow. Each symbol is a burning ember, signifying an app - your social media caldera, your gaming geyser, your newsfeed fumarole. You get to organize them, create categories for topical eruptions, and even alter the backdrop to express your inner fire.

Lava Blaze 2 Home Screen Tips:

- Long press: This reveals a secret menu for each program, allowing you to remove, rename, or transfer it.
- Pinch-to-zoom: Feeling overwhelmed? Zoom out for a bird's-eye perspective of your blazing terrain.
- Widgets: Place mini-apps like weather or news feeds straight on your home screen for at-a-glance updates.
- Quick Settings: Tweaking Your Eruption

Think of fast settings as the volcanic vents of your Lava Blaze 2. Swipe down from the top of your screen to uncover a panel filled with helpful controls. Adjust brightness like a sunbeam dial, activate Wi-Fi like a radio wave transmitter, or blast Bluetooth on like a sonic boom.

Lava Blaze 2 Quick Settings Tips:

Customize Long press on the quick settings panel to rearrange or delete tiles.

- Airplane Mode: One touch disconnects you from all networks, excellent for a digital detox or in-flight rest.
- Power Saver: Feeling the battery drain? Enable battery saving mode to increase your eruption time.
- Notification Center: Where the Ash Settles. The notification center is your Lava Blaze 2's ash cloud, keeping you aware of any action. Social media messages like small flames, calendar alerts like wisps of smoke, and app

updates like volcanic earthquakes - they all converge here.

Lava Blaze 2 Notification Center Tips:

- Clear all: Feeling overwhelmed by the ash? Swipe down with two fingers to delete all alerts in one flaming sweep.

- Priority Notifications: Only want to see the most essential eruptions? Prioritize specific applications to keep their alerts front and center.

- Do Not Disturb: Feeling the heat of continuous notifications? Enable Do Not Disturb to mute the ash cloud for some peace.

Remember, the Lava Blaze 2's dashboard is your portal to its flaming potential. By mastering the home screen, quick settings, and notification center, you become the ultimate eruption commander, wielding your digital volcano with precision and purpose. So go out, explore, and conquer the scorching environment of your Lava Blaze 2!

Connecting the Fire: Wi-Fi, Bluetooth, NFC, and More on Your Lava Blaze 2

Your Lava Blaze 2 isn't just a phone; it's a doorway to a blazing-fast, networked world. But before you can unleash its full power, you need to make some burning bonds. Buckle up, because we're about to dig into the fascinating area of Wi-Fi, Bluetooth, NFC, and other methods to get your Blaze 2 talking.

Wi-Fi: Your Gateway to the Digital Inferno

Imagine a world where information flows like molten lava, and websites explode onto your screen in brilliant colors. That's the power of Wi-Fi! Connecting your Blaze 2 is a breeze:

- ☐ Open the Settings app.
- ☐ Tap on "Network & Internet."
- ☐ Choose "Wi-Fi."
- ☐ Select your selected network and input the password (if any).

And boom! You're in. Now you can surf the web, watch your favorite programs, and download applications at blazing speeds. Remember, a strong Wi-Fi connection is important to an ideal experience. If things are going slow, try moving closer to your router or rebooting your device.

Bluetooth: Sharing the Heat with Other Devices

Bluetooth is like a dependable bridge, connecting your Blaze 2 to a world of wireless possibilities. Want to blast songs on your speakers? No problem! Just link your Blaze 2 with them via Bluetooth. Craving hands-free calling while you jog? Connect your wireless headphones and enjoy the run. Here's how to link your Blaze 2 with another device:

- ☐ Open the Settings app.
- ☐ Tap on "Connected devices."
- ☐ Choose "Bluetooth."

☐ Turn on Bluetooth and make your Blaze 2 discoverable.

☐ Select the device you wish to associate with from the list.

That's it! Now you can exchange music, and files, and even control other devices with your trusty Blaze 2. Remember, Bluetooth has a limited range, so keep your gadgets near for a good connection.

NFC: A One-Tap Inferno of Sharing and Connectivity

Near Field Communication, or NFC, is like a secret handshake for your gadgets. Tap your Blaze 2 against another NFC-enabled device, and things get interesting. You can:

- Share files: Instantly beam images, movies, and contacts to another phone with a single touch.

- Make payments: Skip the wait and pay for things with a single touch at compatible shops.

- Connect to accessories: Pair your Blaze 2 with smart speakers, headphones, and other devices with a simple touch.

To activate NFC on your Blaze 2:

- ☐ Open the Settings app.
- ☐ Tap on "Connected devices."
- ☐ Choose "Connection preferences."
- ☐ Toggle on "NFC."

Now, go ahead and tap! Remember, not all smartphones support NFC, so check before you get too handsy.

Beyond the Basics: Mobile Data and More

Your Blaze 2's connection toolset doesn't end there. You've also got:

- Mobile data: When Wi-Fi isn't accessible, mobile data keeps you connected to the internet, however, it can come at a fee depending on your plan.
- GPS: Get instructions, log your runs, and never get lost again with the built-in GPS.
- USB tethering: Share your Blaze 2's internet connection with other devices like laptops or tablets.

Remember, with tremendous connection comes great responsibility. Use your data sensibly, be cautious of privacy settings, and enjoy the unlimited possibilities that await!

Fueling the Flames: Mastering Battery Management on Your Lava Blaze 2

The Lava Blaze 2 is a technical wonder, a flaming inferno of power and promise. But just like any fire, it requires the correct fuel to keep the flames blazing hot. In this part, we'll dig into the art of battery management, turning you into a master of optimizing charging and prolonging the life of your fiery companion.

Understanding the Fire Within:

Batteries are like small energy stores, and the Lava Blaze 2 holds a strong one. But just like any fuel source, it depletes with time. Understanding the variables that deplete your battery is crucial:

- Display Brightness: This is the largest energy eater. Dimming the screen or enabling auto-brightness considerably increases battery life.
- Apps and Processes: Some apps are more power-hungry than others. Identify battery-draining offenders in your settings and restrict their background activities.
- Connectivity: Constant Wi-Fi, Bluetooth, and GPS use may deplete your battery. Turn them off when not required.
- Push alerts: A steady flood of alerts keeps your CPU humming. Consider restricting

them or utilizing the Do Not Disturb mode.

Optimizing the Charge Cycle

Charging your Lava Blaze 2 correctly is vital for long-term battery health:

- Avoid Excessive Temperatures: Don't charge your phone in excessive heat or cold. Aim for room temperature.
- Partial Charges are Okay: Contrary to common perception, filling up your battery during the day doesn't hurt it.
- Overnight Charging Myth: Leaving your phone plugged in the entire night won't harm the battery, however, newer phones finish charging at 100%. Unplug it to prevent needless wear.

- Use the Right Charger: Stick to the original charger or a high-quality approved substitute.

Extending the Fire's Reign:

Beyond charging, you may modify settings and behaviors to squeeze the most out of your battery:

- Battery Saver Mode: Activate this built-in function to minimize background activities and prolong battery life as required.

- Dark Mode: Many applications provide dark themes, which consume less electricity on OLED panels. Embrace the darkness!

- Location Services: Only allow location access to applications that require it.

- Automatic App Updates: Disable auto-updates for programs you don't use regularly. Update theme manually on Wi-Fi.

- Uninstall Battery Drainers: Identify and delete programs that you seldom use and are renowned for draining the battery.

Bonus Tips:

- Calibrate your battery: This resets the battery level indicator for more accurate readings.

- Turn off vibration: Vibrations consume more power than ringtones.

- Consider a portable charger: For those long days away from an outlet, a power bank is your flaming buddy.

Remember, mastering battery management is a process, not a destination. By studying your use habits, adopting these techniques, and changing your settings, you can keep your Lava Blaze 2 blazing bright, ensuring you always have the strength to dominate your digital world.

Chapter Two

Mastering the Elements

Communication Combustion: Ignite Your Lava Blaze 2's Calling Power

Your Lava Blaze 2 isn't just a phone; it's a communication volcano ready to explode. Let's go into the flaming center of this gadget and examine its arsenal of calling functions, converting you into a master of verbal pyrotechnics.

Making Calls: Setting the Dial Tone Ablaze

- Dialing the Flames: Forget clumsy keypads. Tap a contact, use voice commands like "Hey Blaze, call Mom," or unleash the full potential of your Lava Blaze 2's AI assistant to say things like "Find a plumber near me and call them."

- Speed Dial for Frequent Eruptions: Don't spend time exploring options. Assign your closest contacts to certain numbers on your home screen for rapid scorching connections.

- Conference Call Caldera: Gather your tribe with ease. Initiate multi-party calls and switch between them smoothly, ensuring everyone's voice is heard in the digital firestorm.

Receiving Calls: Answer the Fiery Summons

- Personalized Ringtones: Ditch the bland beeps. Set distinct ringtones for individual callers, so you quickly know who's bursting into your world. Imagine answering your boss's call with a big fanfare, while your sweetheart's ring is a soothing song.

- Call Screening Volcano: Shield yourself from undesired outbursts. Filter calls based on caller ID or even keywords, ensuring only the most critical lava flows reach your ears.

- Visual Voicemail Geysers: No more tiresome voicemail menus. Your Lava Blaze 2 transcribes your communications, converting them into text you can view at your leisure. No more understanding jumbled texts using a phone held perilously to your ear.

Managing Contacts: Your Social Volcano Network

- Sync the Fire: Import your contacts from other smartphones or social networking networks, creating a central crater of connections. No more memorizing a dozen different phonebooks.

- Groups for Eruption Efficiency: Organize your contacts into groups like "Family," "Work Crew," or "Pizza Posse." Send group messages or calls with one swipe, coordinating social eruptions simply.

- Star System for the Brightest Stars: Keep your most critical connections close at hand. Star them for rapid access, guaranteeing they're constantly at the top of your social magma chamber.

Advanced Call Features: Mastering the Pyrotechnics

- Call Recording: Capture critical discussions or humorous moments with the built-in call recorder. Remember that wonderful tale from Aunt Marge? Now you may repeat it on demand.

- Call Forwarding: Divert incoming calls to another number while you're unavailable. No more missing essential calls while you're ascending the mountain of your to-do list.

- Do Not Disturb Mode: Silence the digital rumblings and create a calm retreat. Schedule Do Not Disturb hours to concentrate on activities or just enjoy some peaceful time, away from the continual eruptions of your phone.

Textual Eruptions: Mastering the Lava Blaze 2's Communication Volcano

Your Lava Blaze 2 isn't just a phone; it's a doorway to a universe of textual explosions. SMS, MMS, email, and instant messaging applications are the lava flows of contemporary communication, and understanding them will turn you from a passive spectator to a pyro-linguist – a weaver of words who molds meaning with blazing precision.

- **SMS & MMS: Short Blasts, Big Impact**

Think of SMS and MMS as volcanic ash plumes - quick, sharp bursts that transmit a surprisingly forceful message. Master the skill of producing brief, effective words. Hone your emoji game to add emotional depth, and uncover hidden capabilities like timed messages to surprise your pals with birthday wishes at midnight. For MMS, unleash your inner artist by stacking photos, stickers, and even audio notes on top of your text, creating little multimedia geysers.

- **Email: Channeling the Flow of Information**

Emails are the molten rivers of communication, transporting essential papers, casual thoughts, and everything in between. Tame the email beast by setting up folders and filters to manage the incoming lava flow. Don't be afraid to employ auto-responders for expected situations, and master the keyboard shortcuts that transform you into a typing ninja. Remember, a well-crafted email is like a finely made lava tube — efficient, transparent, and capable of channeling information over huge distances.

- **Instant Messaging: The Pulse of the Social Sphere**

In the volcanic caldera of instant messaging applications, discussions erupt and boil around the clock. Navigate this changing environment with ease by tweaking notification settings to avoid getting buried in ash. Learn the art of the well-timed GIF to infuse fun and spice into your interactions. Master group conversations by leveraging @mentions and polls to keep everyone involved. Remember, in the instant messaging world, brevity is your friend - quick, clever bursts of text keep the discussion flowing like a flaming river.

- **Beyond the Basics: Hacks and Hidden Treasures**

But wait, there's more! Your Lava Blaze 2 contains hidden pathways among these literary volcanoes. Unlock sophisticated features like planned MMS delivery to surprise your loved ones with a morning picture explosion. Utilize text substitution shortcuts to make popular sentences become flaming emojis. Explore third-party keyboard applications to tailor your typing experience with different fonts and themes.

Remember, textual mastery isn't just about knowing the tools; it's about employing them with purpose and creativity. Treat your words like a molten rock - shape them, polish them, and release them onto the world to create literary eruptions that will make a lasting effect. So, fire your Lava Blaze 2, embrace the power of words, and become a master of the literary underworld.

Social Inferno: Navigating the Flames of Social Media on Your Lava Blaze 2

Welcome to the Social Inferno, fellow Lava Blaze 2 wielder! In this digital universe, your phone evolves into a scorching cauldron of connection, innovation, and, well, sometimes mayhem. Fear not, because this book will provide you with the skills and methods to negotiate these flaming platforms and emerge successfully, your social currency surging.

First, pick your battlegrounds:

- Facebook: The OG granddaddy, where family gatherings, pet videos, and fierce political disputes converge. Master the art of the tailored profile, savvy friend requests, and the all-important "Like" to master this ever-evolving beast.

- Instagram: The realm of visually attractive squares, where influencers rule and #foodporn sizzles. Hone your picture editing abilities, add compelling captions, and unleash your inner artist to set your feed ablaze.

- Twitter: A rapid-fire flood of 280-character declarations, where news breaks at the speed of light and memes reign supreme. Learn the art of the clever tweet, the savvy hashtag, and the delicate ballet of following vs. muting to survive this fast-paced firestorm.

- TikTok: The place of viral dances, lip-syncing challenges, and unlimited inventiveness. Unleash your inner performer, master the prevailing trends, and let your individuality show through the 15-second flames.

Now, ready your arsenal:

- Content is king: Share beautiful photographs, informative videos, and engaging tales that generate discussion and inspire curiosity. Remember, quality is above quantity!
- Engage, engage, engage: Like, comment, share, and join in conversations. Be present, be real, and develop meaningful relationships.
- Know your audience: Tailor your material to the platform and your target demographic. What rocks Facebook could fizzle on Twitter.
- Hashtags are your allies: Use relevant hashtags to reach a broader audience and

join the existing debate. But remember, avoid overstuffing!

- Safety first: Be cautious of your privacy settings, look out for fraud and harassment, and remember, the internet is everlasting.

Beyond the flames:

Social media is a tremendous tool, but remember, it's not the only fire in your life. Disconnect to reconnect with the real world, develop offline connections, and recharge your social batteries.

Utilize your phone's built-in capabilities to better your social media game. Edit photographs like a pro with pre-installed tools, schedule posts for best reach, and utilize location tags to highlight your activities. Remember, your Lava Blaze 2 is your ultimate social media weapon, handle it carefully!

So, embrace the flame, fellow social fighter! With these suggestions and your trusty Lava Blaze 2 at your side, you'll cross the Social Inferno with elegance, spark important connections, and emerge triumphant, your social currency hotter than ever!

Multimedia Meltdown: Mastering Your Lava Blaze 2's Creative Inferno

Your Lava Blaze 2 isn't just a phone; it's a pocket-sized multimedia powerhouse poised to explode with spectacular images and immersive sounds. Let's dig into the flaming depths of its camera, editing tools, and entertainment skills, converting you from a casual user to a multimedia maverick.

Photographic Pyrotechnics:

- Unleash the Lens: Your Lava Blaze 2 undoubtedly includes numerous back and front cameras, each with its unique capabilities. Explore wide-angle vistas, get up close with macro images, or shoot gorgeous portraits with bokeh effects. Don't be scared to explore and find your ideal lens for various settings.

- Light the Way: Mastering lighting is vital to mind-blowing pictures. Utilize HDR mode for high-contrast images, dabble with the built-in flash, or seek natural light for a softer touch. Remember, the perfect light may transform an average snap into an outstanding masterpiece.

- Compose with Confidence: Think about the rule of thirds, leading lines, and negative space when framing your images. These fundamental composition methods will add balance and curiosity to your images, making them immediately more attractive.

Editing Like a Pro:

- Built-in Brilliance: Your Lava Blaze 2 undoubtedly comes equipped with excellent editing capabilities. Adjust brightness, contrast, and saturation, trim undesired portions, or add creative effects to customize your photographs and movies.

- Level Up with Applications: Take your editing game to the next level with a multitude of downloadable applications. Enhance colors using VSCO, add creative flare with Snapseed, or make eye-catching collages with Canva. The options are infinite!

- Don't Overdo It: Remember, the idea is to enhance, not mask, your original capture. Go light on the edits, and aim for a natural but striking appearance that matches your style.

Music and Movies: A Feast for the Senses:

- Pump Up the Volume: Your Lava Blaze 2 is a music lover's fantasy. Enjoy high-quality audio with wired or wireless headphones, fire up the songs at a party with its powerful speakers, or lose yourself in a world of customized playlists.

- Cinematic Captivation: Turn your Lava Blaze 2 into a small movie theater. Stream your favorite programs and movies on the move, save material for offline viewing, or even film your cinematic masterpieces with its high-resolution video recording features.

- Immerse Yourself: Don't overlook the power of accessories! Invest in a portable projector to convert any wall into a screen, or purchase a VR headset for really immersive entertainment experiences.

Remember, the key to multimedia expertise is research and experimenting. Don't be afraid to push the limits, release your creativity, and let your Lava Blaze 2 be your canvas for capturing, editing, and enjoying the world around you in spectacular detail and immersive sound. So go out, fire your multimedia enthusiasm, and let the creative flames flare!

Gaming Glory: Level Up Your Mobile Experience with Optimized Settings and Performance Tips

Mobile gaming has become a force in the gaming business, giving the excitement of epic adventures and intense showdowns right in your pocket. But overcoming the digital war involves not only competence but also mastering your gadget. To attain ultimate Gaming Glory, let's dig into the area of optimal settings and performance suggestions to release your phone's hidden potential.

Graphics Tweaks:

- Visual Fidelity: While high-end visuals seem great, they may be taxing. Consider decreasing resolution or visual quality settings for better gaming, particularly on older devices.

- Frame Rate: Targeting a steady 60 frames per second (fps) promotes smooth graphics and responsiveness. Most games offer frame rate choices, emphasize smoothness over eye candy if required.

- Anti-Aliasing: This smooths down rough edges but may be resource-intensive. Try decreasing or deactivating it if you notice frame dips in fast-paced games.

Performance Boosters:

- Resource Management: Close unneeded background programs that consume RAM and CPU resources. Game Boosters incorporated on some phones may automate this procedure.

- Battery Optimization: Battery-saver settings frequently restrict performance. Consider deactivating them when gaming or connecting your phone for continuous power.

- Network Stability: A good Wi-Fi connection is vital for online gaming. If Wi-Fi isn't accessible, prefer a solid 4G/5G data connection to minimize slowness and disconnects.

Touch Controls:

- Sensitivity: Adjust touch sensitivity to reach the sweet spot between responsiveness and inadvertent inputs. Some games give in-game choices for this.

- Virtual Gamepads: Overlay virtual buttons on the screen for more accurate control in FPS or racing games. Many possibilities are accessible via apps or inside certain games.

- Physical Controllers: Invest in a Bluetooth controller for console-like accuracy and comfort, particularly in demanding games.

Beyond the Basics:

- Developer Options: Some phones feature hidden "Developer Options" with additional options. Use them wisely, although settings like "Force 4x MSAA" might further boost visuals on high-end systems.

- Game-Specific advice: Research online groups and forums for game-specific optimization advice. Certain titles could have hidden options or methods to wring out more performance.
- Cooling Solutions: Gaming for lengthy durations may heat your phone, reducing functionality. Portable phone coolers may assist in minimizing thermal throttling, particularly on hot days.

Remember, optimization is a balancing act. Experiment with various options to discover the sweet spot of visual quality, performance, and battery life that matches your device and tastes. Embrace the tinkering spirit, uncover your phone's hidden potential, and climb to gaming greatness!

Chapter Three

Unlocking Hidden Treasures

Customization Crucible: Forging Your Unique Lava Blaze 2 Experience

Your Lava Blaze 2 isn't just a phone; it's an extension of your personality, a link to your digital world. But how can you make it genuinely yours? Enter the Customization Crucible, where we'll build a Lava Blaze 2 that represents your inner fire!

Themes: Painting Your Digital Canvas

Themes are like layers of paint for your phone, quickly modifying its appearance and feel. Craving a sleek, minimalist vibe? Opt for a monochromatic motif with clean lines and subdued tones. Or maybe you're a maximalist at heart? Unleash a brilliant burst of color and patterns.

Remember, themes aren't only visual. Some even modify system icons, fonts, and animations, giving an immersive experience. Explore the Lava Blaze 2 theme shop, or explore third-party alternatives for unlimited possibilities.

Wallpapers: A Window to Your Soul

Your wallpaper is the first thing you see when you burn your Lava Blaze 2. Make it a statement! Nature lovers may luxuriate in stunning vistas, while tech aficionados would choose a metropolis steeped in neon illumination.

For a personal touch, select a revolving background that exhibits your images or artwork. Every time you pick up your phone, it's a small gallery representing your hobbies and memories.

Ringtones & Notifications: Music to Your Ears (and Alerts)

Tired of the same generic notification pings? Craft your soundscape! Assign personalized ringtones for certain contacts, so you quickly know who's calling before even glancing at the screen.

For alerts, pick amusing whistles, futuristic blips, or even grandiose movie music. Make checking your phone an audio excursion! Remember, the appropriate noises may enhance productivity and even decrease stress.

Launchers: Taking Command of Your Home Screen

Launchers are like the captains of your app ecosystem. They determine how you access your favorite programs, widgets, and shortcuts. The default launcher is wonderful, but don't be scared to explore!

Pixel Launcher delivers a clean, Google-centric interface, whereas Nova Launcher allows complete customization options. Experiment with alternative layouts, icon packs, and motions to build a home screen that's as efficient as it is visually beautiful.

Remember, Customization is a Journey, Not a Destination

The beauty of personalization resides in its unlimited possibilities. Don't be scared to explore fresh themes, wallpapers, and launchers.

The ideal arrangement can be only a touch away! As your preferences and demands develop, keep customizing and improving your Lava Blaze 2. Make it a real depiction of your ever-changing digital persona.

So, step into the Customization Crucible and craft your distinctive Lava Blaze 2 experience. Unleash your inner designer, embrace the power of customization, and let your phone become a canvas for your digital creativity!

Productivity Pyrotechnics: Scheduling, Reminders, and Tools to Ignite Your Lava Blaze 2

The Lava Blaze 2 isn't just a phone; it's a productivity powerhouse ready to be unleashed. Forget juggling sticky notes and paper calendars, your beloved gadget holds the secret to conquering your to-do list and becoming a master of time management. Let's go into the burning heart of this digital fire and study the scheduling, reminder, and calendar capabilities that will have you bursting with efficiency.

Scheduling Like a Volcano

- Calendar Crucible: Embrace the built-in calendar app. Schedule appointments, set deadlines, color-code your chores and even sync with your laptop or desktop calendar for seamless organizing. Bonus points for leveraging the Google Calendar connection for powerful scheduling across devices.

- Alarms Ablaze: Don't miss a beat! Set recurring or single alarms, tweak their sounds and snooze lengths, and mark them for certain tasks. Imagine waking up to the calm chirping of "Finish that report!" instead of the startling blare of a generic alarm.

- Reminders that Rock: Let your Lava Blaze 2 spark your memory. Set location-based reminders that ding you when you arrive at the grocery store or the gym. Time-based reminders guarantee you never forget that dental appointment or essential call again.

Taming the To-Do Tempest:

- Task Eruptions: Tame the to-do monster with tools like Google Tasks or Microsoft

To Do. Create lists, prioritize chores, assign due dates, and mark them accomplished as you tackle them. Bonus points for integrating with project management systems like Asana or Trello for total task supremacy.

- Habitual Heatwaves: Want to establish beneficial habits? Apps like Streaks or Habitica gamify the process. Track your progress, get incentives, and remain inspired to conquer your objectives, one healthy habit at a time.

Tools to Fuel Your Focus:

- Digital Detox Dome: Feeling swamped by notifications? Utilize settings like Do Not Disturb and Focus Mode to hush the digital buzz and give yourself designated periods of undisturbed time. Imagine a quiet refuge among the notification tempest, enabling you to sink deep into concentrated work.

- App Avalanche Blocker: Identify and manage time-sucking applications. Set use restrictions or schedule app blocks to eliminate aimless browsing and guarantee you remain laser-focused on the subject at hand. Your attention is a valuable resource; defend it hard!

Remember:

- Personalize Your Inferno: Experiment with various applications and tools to get the right productivity concoction that matches your workstyle and tastes. Your

Lava Blaze 2 is your canvas; create your route to maximum efficiency!

- Embrace the Flow: Don't be scared to change your system as required. Listen to your productivity cycles and alter your calendar, reminders, and tools to develop a system that keeps you flowing like molten lava.

By utilizing the power of the Lava Blaze 2's scheduling, reminder, and productivity capabilities, you can change from a chaotic mess to a focused, efficient machine. Remember, it's not about conquering every minute; it's about spending your time wisely and making the most of your blazing potential. So, fire your Lava Blaze 2, release the productive pyrotechnics inside, and see your ambitions explode into reality!

Security Shield: Protecting Your Data with Passwords, Encryption, and Anti-Malware Solutions

In today's digital age, our data is more precious than ever. From personal information like bank accounts and social security numbers to beloved memories and creative labor, our smartphones carry a treasure mine of sensitive information. But with tremendous ease comes great responsibility, the need to secure our data from illegal access, theft, and harmful assaults.

This is where our Security Shield comes in. Imagine a three-pronged fortification shielding your digital assets: strong passwords, unbreakable encryption, and attentive anti-malware solutions.

Passwords are the first line of defense, the guardians of your digital domain. But weak passwords are like flimsy doors - readily knocked down by determined burglars. Here's how to design a password powerhouse:

- Complexity is key: Ditch the dictionary terms and birthdates! Opt for a combination of capital and lowercase characters, numerals, and symbols. Think "P@ssw0rd123" to "P@r@d0x1c@l_Sh!3ld."

- Uniqueness is crucial: Don't reuse the same password for several accounts. A single breach might leave all your data vulnerable. Imagine using the same key for your house, vehicle, and bank vault — not a smart idea!

- Password managers are your allies: They create and store strong, unique passwords for all your accounts, making them a security must-have.

Encryption Enigma:

Encryption scrambles your data into an unreadable code, rendering it worthless to anybody without the decryption key. Think of it as a secret language only you and the authorized receiver understand.

- Data at rest and in transit: Encrypt your vital data, photographs, and documents at rest (stored on your device) and in transit (transmitted over the internet). Imagine transmitting critical papers via a secured briefcase instead of an open envelope.
- HTTPS is your friend: Look for the "https" in site URLs, indicating a secure

connection protected using HTTPS protocol. It's like having a secure tunnel for your online conversation.

Anti-Malware Arsenal

Malware, the harmful software hiding in the digital shadows, may steal your data, commandeer your gadgets, and cause havoc. Anti-malware solutions are your knights in shining armor, continually checking for and eliminating these dangers.

- Keep your guard up: Install and routinely update trusted anti-malware software on all your devices. Think of it as having a security guard monitoring your digital border.
- Be careful online: Don't click on strange links or download files from unfamiliar sources. These may be Trojan horses

conveying malware in disguise. Imagine a friendly-looking present package holding a bomb — always be aware of unexpected digital gifts!

- Regular scans are essential: Schedule regular scans to identify and remove any malware that could have slipped through the gaps. Think of it as a full security scan of your digital citadel.

By constructing a comprehensive Security Shield with strong passwords, encryption, and anti-malware technologies, you can safely traverse the digital world, knowing your important data is secure and sound. Remember, your data is your castle - protect it with the toughest of digital knights!

Cracking the Code: Hidden Features and Easter Eggs of the Lava Blaze 2

Beyond the surface of your sleek Lava Blaze 2 lies a hidden universe of secret functions and delightful surprises. Think of it as a digital Narnia, ready to be opened by intrepid explorers like you. Ditch the ordinary, grab your curiosity, and let's plunge into the hot core of your phone, finding its hidden gems:

1. Shazam on Steroids: Tired of humming a track without knowing its name? Double-press the power button (yes, really!), and your Lava Blaze 2 morphs into a supersonic Shazam. It'll detect the tune even in a crowded bazaar, feeding your musical demands promptly.

2. The Camera Chameleon: Unleash your inner photographer with hidden camera settings. Swipe down rapidly on the volume rocker while in the camera app, and voilà! You've unlocked "Long Exposure," great for capturing lovely light trails and ethereal water blurs. For those action-packed moments, swipe up twice — say welcome to "Burst Mode," taking rapid-fire pictures to freeze even the quickest hummingbird's wings.

3. The Battery Whisperer: Anxious about juice levels? Dial ##4636#*# and a hidden menu opens up. Dive into "Battery Information," where you'll discover hidden treasures like "Signal Strength" - adjust your connection to increase battery life. Pro tip: activate "Show Battery Percentage" under Developer Options for real-time juice updates.

4. The Code Cracker: Feeling cryptic? Dial ##83781#*# to enter "Engineering Mode." Don't worry, most alternatives are innocuous. Play with "Vibration Test" to feel your phone tremble like a mini-earthquake, or investigate "Network Information" to become a data-savvy investigator. Remember, with tremendous power comes great responsibility — tread wisely.

5. The Easter Egg Hunt: Remember the pleasure of childhood hunts? Your Lava Blaze 2 conceals fun easter eggs too! Open the Settings app, click on "About Phone," and touch "Lava Version" repeatedly. A burning emblem appears up - keep touching until a lava lamp animation greets you, followed by a relaxing crackling. Relax, you've calmed the digital flames!

Bonus Tip: Keep your eyes peeled for updates! Lava Labs enjoys sliding in new hidden features with each software version. Explore forums, join online communities, and become a Lava Blaze 2 whisperer, sharing your discoveries with other fiery adventurers.

Connecting to the Lava Universe: Downloading Apps, Google Play, and Staying Updated

Welcome to the vibrant ecosystem of the Lava Blaze 2! Beyond its built-in features lies a vast expanse of possibilities waiting to be explored through the gateway of apps. This chapter serves as your compass, guiding you through the exciting world of app downloads, navigating the Google Play Store like a pro, and ensuring your Lava Blaze 2 stays at the forefront of innovation.

Imagine your Lava Blaze 2 as a blank canvas, ready to be splashed with the vibrant colors of your passions and interests. Apps are the paintbrushes, transforming your device into a productivity powerhouse, an entertainment haven, or a personalized portal to your hobbies.

Downloading apps is a breeze:

- Open the Google Play Store: It's usually pre-installed on your Lava Blaze 2, easily identifiable by its colorful triangle icon.

- Explore or Search: Feeling adventurous? Browse curated app categories or themed collections. Know what you want? Utilize the powerful search bar to find specific apps.

- Tap to Install: Once you've found the perfect app, tap the "Install" button. Sit back and relax as your Lava Blaze 2 downloads and installs the app, ready for you to unleash its potential.

Mastering the Google Play Store: Your Personal App Curator

The Google Play Store isn't just a marketplace; it's your curator, recommending apps you might love based on your usage and interests. Let's delve deeper into its functionalities:

- My apps & games: Keep track of your downloaded apps, update them, and uninstall any that no longer spark joy.
- Wishlist: Craft a wish list for future app adventures, ensuring you never miss out on the latest must-haves.

- Parental Controls: Keep your family safe by setting app download restrictions and age-appropriate content filters.

- Offers & Deals: Score amazing discounts and freebies on popular apps, maximizing the value of your Lava Blaze 2 experience.

Staying Updated: Ensuring Your Lava Blaze 2 Blazes Brightly

Just like your favorite game, apps receive regular updates to improve performance, fix bugs, and introduce new features. Keeping your apps updated is crucial for optimal performance and security:

- Enable auto-update: Let your Lava Blaze 2 handle the heavy lifting by enabling auto-updates for apps. You'll always have the latest versions without lifting a finger.

- Manual updates: Prefer to be in control? Head over to "My apps & games" and tap "Update" next to the apps you want to refresh.

- System updates: Your Lava Blaze 2 itself receives periodic system updates to enhance stability and security. Stay notified and install updates promptly to keep your device at its best.

Chapter Four

Taming the Wildfire (Troubleshooting)

Common Eruptions: Taming the Everyday Tech Volcano

Your Lava Blaze 2 is a technological marvel, a pocket inferno of power and possibility. But even the mightiest volcano can experience the occasional tremor. Fear not, intrepid user, for this guide will equip you to diagnose and quell the most common eruptions plaguing your Blaze 2: Wi-Fi woes, app avalanches, and battery drain droughts.

- Wi-Fi Woes: Your internet connection sputtering like a damp firework? First, ensure the router is powered and online. A simple reboot can often work wonders. Check for network congestion; too many devices vying for bandwidth can cause sluggishness. Consider switching to a 5GHz band for less interference. If problems persist, scan for available networks, ensuring you're connected to the correct one. Resetting network settings on your Blaze 2 can be a last resort, but remember to back up essential passwords beforehand.

- App Avalanches: Apps crashing can feel like a meteor shower raining on your productivity. Start by identifying the culprit. Has a single app gone rogue, or are multiple apps misbehaving? If it's one app, try clearing its cache and data. If that doesn't work, consider uninstalling and reinstalling it. For widespread app crashes, check for software updates on your Blaze 2. Outdated software can lead to compatibility issues. Force-rebooting your device can also clear temporary glitches. In extreme cases, a factory reset might be necessary, but remember, this erases all user data, so backup diligently.

- Battery Drain Droughts: A sluggish battery feels like lava turning lukewarm. First, analyze your habits. Are you a chronic screen-scroller, a location-tracking enthusiast, or a Bluetooth-loving music fiend? These features are power-hungry dragons. Optimize settings by lowering screen brightness, disabling location services when not needed, and limiting background app activity. Consider battery-saving mode for extended journeys. Check for rogue apps draining the battery unexpectedly; uninstall any culprits. Lastly, ensure your power cable and adapter are functioning properly. If battery concerns persist, consider replacing the battery itself.

Remember, even the most knowledgeable users encounter tech tremors. Stay calm, follow these steps, and soon your Lava Blaze 2 will be erupting with its full potential once more. For more advanced eruptions, consulting Lava Blaze 2's official support resources or seeking professional help is always wise. With the right tools and knowledge, you can turn any tech tremor into a learning opportunity and keep your Lava Blaze 2 burning bright.

Advanced Troubleshooting: Taming the Digital Inferno

Even the fiercest Lava Blaze 2 can occasionally cough up smoke. When common fixes fizzle out and your frustration builds like a volcanic eruption, fear not, for this chapter equips you with the tools to tackle the fiercest digital dragons.

Delving into the Darkness:

- Boot Camp Blues: Stuck on a frozen screen? Try a forced reboot: hold down the power and volume buttons for 10-15 seconds. If the lava refuses to flow, connect to a charger and hold both buttons again. Still cold? Contact support – there might be deeper magma issues.

- App Abyss: Is a single app causing chaos? Boot into safe mode (restart while holding volume down) to diagnose. If peace reigns in this barren landscape, the culprit resides within the app itself. Uninstall and reinstall, update, or seek alternative apps.

- Performance Peril: Is your Blaze 2 slowing down like molasses in winter? Close background apps, clear cached data (Settings > Storage > Apps), and update all software. Consider a factory reset as a last resort, but remember, this is a fiery baptism – all data will be incinerated. Back it up first!

Software Sorcery:

- Update Inferno: Updates can be blessings or curses. Before hitting "install," check online forums and reviews for potential downsides. If your Blaze 2 is behaving unpredictably after an update, you can (sometimes) roll back to a previous version. Contact support for guidance on this advanced maneuver.

- Rooting Rampage: Rooting unlocks hidden potential, but tread carefully. Incorrect modifications can brick your device. Research extensively, understand the risks, and back up everything before venturing into this volcanic terrain. Remember, warranty spells might go up in smoke with rooting.

Factory Reset Ritual:

- The Last Resort: When all else fails, the factory reset looms large. This fiery purge erases everything, returning your Blaze 2 to its pristine, out-of-the-box state. Make sure you've backed up your data and photos, as once unleashed, this reset cannot be undone.

Erupting with Confidence: Mastering the Lava Support System

Lava Blaze 2 isn't just a device, it's an inferno of possibilities. But even the hottest flames sometimes flicker. Fear not, intrepid Blaze 2 user, for when embers of doubt smolder, the Lava Support System stands ready to reignite your tech journey. This guide will equip you with the tools to conquer any obstacle, so buckle up and prepare to blaze through a seamless support experience.

Reaching the Volcano's Heart: Contacting Customer Service

- Dialing the Hot Line: Nothing beats a good old-fashioned phone call. Dial the dedicated Lava Blaze 2 support line and speak directly to a friendly, knowledgeable agent. Remember, patience is key, for even fiery assistance can take a moment to heat up.

- Live Chat Eruption: Feeling the need for instant solutions? Hop onto the Live Chat feature on the Lava website. Converse with a support agent in real time, watch flames of understanding flicker on the screen, and extinguish your tech woes before they turn into ash.

- Emailing the Ash Clouds: Sometimes, the written word works best. Craft a detailed email outlining your issue and send it to Lava's dedicated support email address. Lava agents, like volcanic warriors, will dissect your query, analyze its molten core, and send a solution erupting back into your inbox.

Exploring the Lava Lands: Finding Online Resources

- Knowledge Base Odyssey: Venture into the vast Knowledge Base, a library of wisdom guarded by wise Lava experts. Search for keywords, peruse FAQs, and unearth volcanic nuggets of knowledge that brighten even the deepest tech caves.
- Video Tutorials: Watch the Flames Dance: Sometimes, seeing is believing. Lava's video tutorials take you step-by-step through common tasks and solutions, like calming the fiery rage of a buggy app or optimizing your battery's volcanic lifespan.

- Forum Fellowship: Don't go it alone! Join the Lava forum, a community of intrepid Blaze 2 users sharing tips, tricks, and stories of their tech experiences. Post your inquiry and observe the geysers of helpful advice erupt from other travelers.

Unleashing the Full Potential: Getting the Help You Need

- Be Prepared with Lava: Before calling help, assemble your armament. Note down error messages, model numbers, and other pertinent facts that can assist in identifying the problem. The more information you supply, the sooner the Lava agents can send the cavalry roaring in.

- Clarity is Key: Articulate your problem simply and succinctly. Explain your symptoms, not simply the diagnosis. Remember, even the greatest Lava agents can't read minds, so the clearer you are, the faster the answer will come.

- Patience is Lava Gold: Tech issues might be irritating, but remember, the Lava Support System is intended to assist, not criticize. Breathe deeply, keep cool, and believe that the fiery answers are on their way.

With these tools at your fingertips, navigating the Lava Support System will be a snap. Remember, even the brightest tech fires occasionally require a helping hand to stay blazing bright. So, embrace the explosion, overcome your tech troubles, and unleash the full power of your Lava Blaze 2 with confidence. You are the lord of your digital fires, and the Lava Support System is your volcanic ally, always ready to lead you through the hot terrain of technology.

Chapter Five

Unleashing the Full Potential

Power User Playground: Unleashing the Lava Blaze 2's Inner Inferno

Welcome, Lava Blaze 2 masters, to the flaming center of the gadget - the Power User Playground. Here, we lay off the training wheels and dive into the secret depths of your digital companion, changing it from a reliable tool into a burning extension of your will. Automation, sophisticated settings, and performance optimization await, ready to adapt your Lava Blaze 2 to your exact demands and spark your productivity like never before.

Automation: Your Fiery Familiar

Imagine directing your Lava Blaze 2 with the strength of your voice, like a mythological dragon speaking commands to its flaming breath. With task automation tools, you may create unique routines that perform repetitive activities with a single phrase or button push. Craving the ideal morning ritual? Automate turning on lights, preparing coffee, and playing your favorite power anthem as you wake.

Feeling swamped by emails? Set up auto-filters and answers to tame the inbox beast. The possibilities are boundless, like a personal genie educated in the art of digital efficiency.

Advanced Settings: Tweaking the Flames
Venture beyond the familiar UI and uncover the hidden lair of advanced options. Here, you may fine-tune your Lava Blaze 2 to behave like a

beautifully tuned race vehicle. Want to squeeze every drop of battery life? Dive into power management choices and deactivate power-hungry background programs. Craving top gaming performance? Unchain the graphics processor and unleash the full fury of your favorite games. Remember, with great power comes great responsibility, so step cautiously and explore these settings with a passion for information and a good dose of caution.

Optimizing for the Forge:

Every user's demands are unique, and the Lava Blaze 2 bends to your will like molten metal. Whether you're a social media fanatic, a productivity warrior, or a creative thinker, customize your device for your workflow. Photographers may modify picture processing settings for astonishing clarity, writers can arrange keyboard shortcuts for lightning-fast creativity, and social media gurus can tune alerts and data consumption to remain connected without exhausting the battery. The goal is to determine your requirements, examine the various possibilities, and experiment until your Lava Blaze 2 seems like an extension of your mind.

Remember, the Power User Playground is not only about technical capability, it's about creativity and discovery. Don't be afraid to explore, adjust, and customize your Lava Blaze 2 until it represents your distinct digital fingerprint. Share your findings with other power users, develop a community of ardent tech enthusiasts, and together, push the frontiers of what this extraordinary technology can achieve.

Pro Tips & Tricks: Hacking Your Way to Productivity, Entertainment, and User Nirvana Ready to unleash the inner ninja of your Lava Blaze 2? Buckle up, because we're going into the world of expert tips and tactics that'll accelerate your productivity, improve your enjoyment, and convert your user experience into a symphony of seamless efficiency.

Productivity Pyrotechnics:

Automate the Inferno: Forget laborious jobs! Schedule emails, messages, and even social network posts to go live as you conquer other realms. Use IFTTT for automated routines like switching on Wi-Fi when you come home or silencing calls during meetings.

Split-screen Sorcery: Master multitasking with split-screen mode. Work on projects while checking up on emails, watch lessons while taking notes, all with a flick of your wrist.

Focus Like a Phoenix: Silence distractions! Enable Do Not Disturb, set Focus Mode to disable particular applications during work hours, and even transform your Lava Blaze 2 into a grayscale productivity powerhouse.

Gesture Mastery: Forget typing, swipe your way to success! Master secret motions like pinching to zoom in applications, drawing patterns to activate certain actions, or shaking your phone to undo.

Entertainment Eruption:

- Audio Alchemy: Transform your Lava Blaze 2 into a soundscape! Download Dolby Atmos applications for immersive audio, modify equalization settings for your favorite genres, and even employ Bluetooth codecs for lossless audio on wireless headphones.

- Gaming Glory: Unleash the inner gamer! Use game boosters for speedier gaming, modify graphics settings for best performance, and even connect external controllers for console-like experiences.

- Hidden Cinema: Discover hidden methods to view movies and series. Download offline copies for airport journeys, cast your screen to TVs for big-screen adventures, and discover streaming services with localized content to open a world of entertainment.

- Personalization Playground: Craft your digital sanctuary! Use custom fonts, live wallpapers, and icon packs to customize your interface. Theme your phone around your favorite movies, games, or hobbies to completely own your digital environment.

User Experience Nirvana:

- Hidden Shortcuts: Unlock the hidden code! Learn keyboard shortcuts for rapid tasks, swipe motions for navigation, and even voice commands for hands-free control.

- Accessibility Ascension: Make your Lava Blaze 2 work for you! Enable options like high contrast mode, font resizing, and voice aid for increased reading and ease of use.

- Night Vision Magic: Turn your Lava Blaze 2 into a friendly companion for late-night escapades. Enable Night Light to limit blue light output, schedule automatic dimming, and even modify color temperature for warmer, sleep-inducing tones.

- Data Detox Delight: Reclaim your digital detox! Track app use, establish data limitations, plan digital downtime, and even deploy website blocks to recover your attention and mental wellness.

Remember, they are only sparks to fire your imagination. Explore forums, online groups, and app stores to unearth even more hidden possibilities. Remember, your Lava Blaze 2 is a canvas, and you're the artist. So go out, hack your way to productivity, enjoyment, and user experience nirvana, and let your inner tech ninja shine!

The Future of Lava Blaze 2: Where the Flames Rise Higher

The Lava Blaze 2 has already lit your digital world ablaze, but strap up because the heat's going to kick up a notch. Lava isn't resting on its fiery laurels, and the future contains new improvements, features, and innovations that will make your Blaze 2 even more formidable. So, let's plunge into the flames and see what's brewing:

1. AI on Steroids: Get ready for an even smarter Blaze 2. Advanced AI algorithms will power features like context-aware suggestions, hyper-personalized app recommendations, and predictive battery management. Imagine your phone anticipating your requirements before you even thought about them!

2. Unleashing the Camera Beast: Prepare to be shocked by next-level photography and filming. Expect AI-powered scene optimization, automated noise reduction, and cinematic video stabilization that'll make your shaky handheld footage appear like Hollywood magic. Get ready to become a social media master!

3. Gaming Inferno: Brace yourself for a mobile gaming revolution. The future Blaze 2 promises better refresh rates, greater graphics rendering, and specialized gaming modes that'll push your games to the stratosphere. Multiplayer combat will be smoother, more engaging, and leave your opponents in the dust.

4. The linked Ecosystem: Lava envisions a completely linked environment where your

Blaze 2 is the key hub. Smart home integration, wearables that increase health and fitness monitoring, and frictionless data transmission across devices will offer a comprehensive digital experience beyond your wildest expectations.

5. Security Forged in Lava: Stay ahead of the digital bad guys with cutting-edge security technologies. Biometric authentication will grow even more advanced, data encryption will be impregnable, and real-time threat detection will keep your important information secure from damage. Sleep well knowing your digital fortress is unbreachable.

Staying Ahead of the Curve:

To become a Lava Blaze 2 master, don't simply wait for the upgrades to pour in. Be proactive!

- Join the Lava Community: Get exclusive information, engage in beta testing, and connect with other Blaze 2 lovers.

- Follow Lava on social media: Stay up-to-date on the latest news, announcements, and sneak previews of planned features.

- Explore online resources: Blogs, forums, and tech channels commit themselves to maximizing the Blaze 2's capabilities. Dive in and learn from the professionals.

- Enroll in online courses: Hone your abilities and access hidden features with specialized courses aimed at power users.

Personalizing Your Fire: Building a Lava Blaze 2 Experience Tailored to You

Your Lava Blaze 2 isn't just a phone; it's a doorway to your digital inferno. It dances to your beat, crackles with your passions, and bursts with your creation. But with so many adjustable possibilities, where do you start? Buckle up, because we're about to ignite your Lava Blaze 2 experience and forge it into a mirror of your unique personality.

Fueling the Furnace with Themes:

First, paint your digital flames with themes! Are you a nature lover? Immerse yourself in beautiful landscapes and tranquil waterfalls. A minimalist aesthetic in your jam? Craft a sleek, tidy workstation. Craving a bright cyberpunk vibe? Go full-on Tron with vivid grids and flashing symbols. Remember, your topic is your canvas, so unleash your inner artist!

Widgets: Shortcuts to Your Passions:

Widgets are like small volcanoes, exploding with rapid access to the things you love. News junkie? Have news simmering on your home screen. Fitness fanatic? Track your steps with a blazing dashboard. Musician? Let your playlist fire with a simple touch. Every widget is a customized explosion, pushing your interests closer to the surface.

Automation: The Lava Flows for You:

Imagine never rushing for your headphones again. With automation, your Lava Blaze 2 anticipates your demands. Set it to automatically switch to quiet mode during classes, blast your exercise soundtrack as you enter the gym, or lower the lights for nighttime reading. Let everyday duties transform like automatic lava flows, enabling you to seek your inner ambitions.

Ringtones & Notifications: Your Sonic Signature:

Don't settle with generic beeps! Craft a unique symphony of noises that greets your arrival. A booming guitar riff for calls, a fun melody for texts, and a triumphal fanfare for arriving emails. Make your alerts an extension of your personality, a sound identity that screams, "This is me, loud and proud!"

Beyond the Surface: Apps that Stoke Your Fire:

The app store is your geyser, filled with tools and experiences ready to be tapped. Whether you're a budding photographer, a code warrior, or a language genius, there's an app to light your fires. Discover hidden jewels that

Remember, your Lava Blaze 2 is a blank canvas, ready for your touch. Don't be hesitant to explore, adjust, and develop your digital world. Let your interests lead your adaptations, and let your creativity explode like a stunning volcanic show. This isn't just a phone; it's your inferno, blazing bright with your unique fire of you.